HAYNES EXPLAINS
BABIES

Owners' Workshop Manual

© Haynes Publishing • Written by **Boris Starling**

Published in October 2016

A catalogue record for this book is available from the British Library

ISBN 078 1 78521 102 7

Haynes Publishing, Sparkford, Yeovil, Somerset BA22 7JJ, UK
Tel: +44 (0) 1963 440635
Website: www.haynes.com

Haynes North America, Inc.,
861 Lawrence Drive, Newbury Park, California 91320, USA

Printed and bound in Malaysia

Cover image from Getty Images

Written by **Boris Starling**
Edited by **Louise McIntyre**
Designed by **Richard Parsons**

Safety first!

It is imperative to adhere to certain stringent safety measures with babies. In some cases, the very existence of the baby may signal a disregard for precautions approximately nine months previously.

a) Always cradle the baby's head when picking him up or holding him.

b) Always ensure that the baby's in sight or can't escape from where you've left him: Houdini had nothing on the average infant.

c) Always wear clothes you don't mind looking and smelling like a sewage worker's uniform.

Working facilities

Optimal working space for babies is in direct and inverse proportion to their size. For example, a baby boy 12 weeks old who is 60cm long and weighs 6kg will need approximately 12km^2 – the size of Heathrow, more or less – to accommodate all their toys, prams, nappy-changing facilities, clothes, sterilisers and so on. By the time this boy is 18 and almost two metres tall, he will be able to fit everything he owns into a small backpack. Go figure.

Contents

Introduction

Welcome to *Haynes Explains: Babies*. There are few events that can truly be described as life-changing – even 'see Naples and die' now applies more to the locals' driving than the city's beauty – but having a baby is definitely one of them. Before your first baby arrives, you may think it will be rather like a pet: hard work, sure, but fundamentally easy to deal with as long as you offer food and love. Most of all, you're sure you will be in control.

You will realise how wrong you were no later than 12 hours after giving birth. This tiny creature will take over your life like a cross between a sci-fi movie alien and a medieval tyrant.

a) It will regurgitate over you from all available orifices.

b) It will keep you awake into the small hours.

c) It will introduce you to a lifetime of worry.

d) It will never say 'please' or 'thank you'.

e) Its table manners will make a pig look as refined as Brian Sewell.

f) And you will love it with a passion and ferocity that can sometimes seem almost frightening in their intensity.

Welcome to parenthood.
Prepare to have your world rocked.

About this manual

The aim of this manual is to help you get the best value from your Baby. It can do this in several ways. It can help you (a) decide what work must be done (b) tackle this work yourself, though you may choose to have much of it performed by external contractors such as grandparent, a nanny, or That Woman Down The Road Who Only Charges A Fiver An Hour.

The manual has drawings and descriptions to show the function and layout of the various components. Tasks are described in a logical order so that even a novice can do the work, which should prove useful to those whose brains have been turned to porridge by the relentless demands of pandering to every whim of a pint-sized milk-fuelled tyrant. Life does get easier, even though you may not think so when it's 3.30am and you're so tired you can't even remember your own name.

Dimensions, weights and capacities

Overall height (average, 9 months)
Baby (Blue Model) 68.2cm
Baby (Pink Model)...................................... 67.0cm
Both Blue and Pink models grow so fast in the first year that
you'll swear they do it deliberately when you're not looking.

Kerb weight (average, 9 months)
Baby (Blue Model) 7.4kg
Baby (Pink Model)...................................... 7.4kg

Capacities
For milk .... bottomless
For sleep .... intermittent, always out of sync with you
For filling nappies .... has to be seen to be believed

Liquid refuelling, quantities and intervals
0–2 months .... 90ml every 2 hours
3–4 months .... 150ml every 3 hours
5–6 months .... 220ml every 5 hours

Maximum acceleration
When crying .... from silent to 120db: 0.0036 seconds
When crawling .... from safety to hazardous situation: 3.29s

Engine
Stroke .... rubbing their backs after feeding
Power... 168bhp ('burping high performance'
.... rather than 'brake horsepower.')
Torque .... 278lb ft (where objects being twisted
.... = dog's tail in manic baby hands)
Redline .... easily accessed when tired and hungry

Assembly

The assembly phase lasts nine months and is usually broken down into three trimesters of three months each. Their formal names are first trimester, second trimester and third trimester, but they are usually known as Sick and Tired, Baby Kicks Are So Cute, and Had Enough Now Get On With It.

Nine months is also the time it takes to reach Mars from Earth. There will be occasions when a ticket to the Red Planet will seem a pretty decent swap.

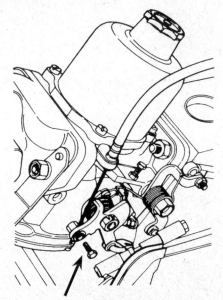

FIG 1•1 **AN ILL-CONSIDERED SCREW, CONSEQUENCES CAN BE DRASTIC**

⚠ General pregnancy tips

1) If a woman is pregnant over Valentine's Day and says that this baby is the only present she needs, she is lying.

2) Men may choose to develop a bump in sympathy and solidarity with their partner. A regular application of cheeseburgers, kebabs and lager should ensure smooth progress in this regard.

3) Many pregnant women like to take extra supplements. Vitamin D, folic acid, iron and calcium are all good. Anabolic steroids are bad: they'll cause facial hair, acne and a deep voice, and your man should have all of these covered himself. On the plus side, he won't see which way you went in the 100 metres.

⚠ First Trimester

You may not look pregnant during the first trimester, but your body is going through enormous changes. Your hormone levels, blood supplies and heart rate will all increase. These changes are responsible for many of the symptoms of early pregnancy like fatigue, headaches and morning sickness. A single enjoyable night which makes you feel grotty for a long time afterwards: basically, the first trimester is one long hangover, which is ironic given that alcohol's the first thing off the menu.

Things you may discover:

1) Morning sickness was clearly named by a man, as it can continue way beyond midday: at least until *Countdown* and sometimes all the way to *Coronation Street*.

2) Hamlet didn't know whether to be or not to be. You may ask yourself whether to pee or not to pee. Pee. Always.

3) You will have food cravings too weird to be explained by any rational molecular gastronomic science. Pilchards with vanilla ice cream, chalk with dry teabags, chocolate cake with pickled onions, the mud off unwashed potatoes – these are all real cravings reported by women in their first trimester.

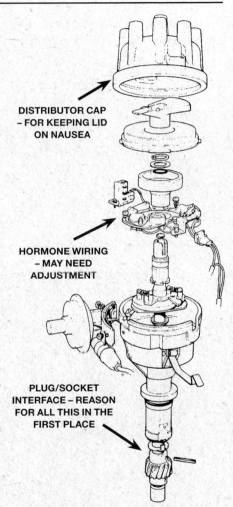

DISTRIBUTOR CAP – FOR KEEPING LID ON NAUSEA

HORMONE WIRING – MAY NEED ADJUSTMENT

PLUG/SOCKET INTERFACE – REASON FOR ALL THIS IN THE FIRST PLACE

FIG 1•2 **DISTRIBUTOR, EXPLODED VIEW – INTERNAL WORKINGS UNDERSTOOD ONLY BY PROFESSIONALS**

Second Trimester

The second trimester is almost always the most comfortable. Many of the early symptoms will disappear, and you will have more energy in the daytime and sleep better at night.

The 12-week scan, which heralds the transition from first to second trimester, is also the sign for you to start telling friends and colleagues (you may have told your families earlier, though then again you may not have if your family is more Addams than Partridge.) Besides, you will now start to look pregnant.

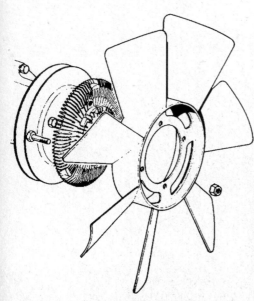

FIG 1•3 **YOUR NUMBER 1 FAN**

Things you may discover:

1) Male partners who say 'we're pregnant'. No, mate. We are not anything. She is pregnant. He is walking round all smug that he's not firing blanks. Think of the difference between involvement and commitment. When it comes to eggs, a chicken is involved: when it comes to bacon, a pig is committed. In this pregnancy, the man is the chicken.

2) There may be awkward moments when others vacillate between buying you a babygro or a gym membership, or when you hear someone whisper 'blimey, she's let herself go a bit, hasn't she?'

3) If your nesting instinct sends you venturing into the maternity sections of department stores, beware the 'baby advisors'. They are not there to offer advice. They are there to sell the hell out of a ton of stuff you won't need.

Waiting for your baby to arrive is like picking someone up from the airport without knowing who they are or what time their flight lands.

⚠ Third Trimester

You will see your doctor more frequently during the third trimester as the due date approaches. The doctor will check your blood pressure, listen to your baby's heart rate, check the baby's position and so on. You may also choose to enrol in a childbirth class, where you can set not just your watch but the atomic clock by the nanosecond between the instructor starting the video of an actual childbirth and all the men in the room turning green and sprinting for the door while muttering something about having to call the office.

Things you may discover:

1) Every month has between 28 and 31 days except for the ninth month of pregnancy, which has 6483.

2) You will not want to go out in the evening so much, giving your partner a pink ticket for the last time in a while. Men: this pink ticket most definitely has an expiry date. Use it or lose it.

3) People will tell you that leggings or tracksuit bottoms aren't trousers. At nine months gone, trousers are whatever you say they are.

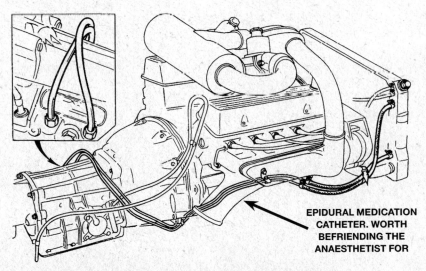

EPIDURAL MEDICATION CATHETER. WORTH BEFRIENDING THE ANAESTHETIST FOR

FIG 1·4 **SOPHISTICATED PAIN-REDUCTION MACHINERY. CAN MINIMISE ALL ANNOYANCES EXCEPT HUSBANDS**

Production

The day is almost upon you. Birthing plans have been written and revised. A suitcase is packed and sitting by the door like that of a Soviet dissident waiting for the knock from the KGB. The car is filled with petrol, the route to hospital is burned into the sat-nav's electronic brain. You and your partner are a well-oiled machine waiting to spring into action the moment you feel your first contraction. But, as any soldier will tell you, no plan survives first contact with the enemy.

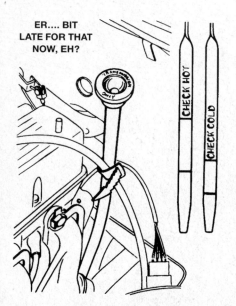

ER.... BIT LATE FOR THAT NOW, EH?

CHECK HOT

CHECK COLD

FIG 1•5 **DIPSTICK TEST FOR HCG TRACES IN URINE**

When is labour not labour?

If your answer includes the words 'Tony Blair', go to the back of the class. When it's a Braxton Hicks practice contraction. Braxton Hicks should not be confused with either Branston Pickle or the Higgs-Boson particle, though both may have already featured during your labour as weird food craving and bored-of-waiting timewarp sensation respectively.

Labour

When labour starts in earnest, it's game face on, all hands on deck and any other number of mixed metaphors. Half a century ago, a father might not even have left the office, except to go to the pub with his colleagues and raise a jar to his potency. Now he's expected to be at the maternal bedside throughout.

Some women like their man to press a rolling pin against their back to help relieve the pressure. Men who overdo the rolling pin may find

a) That it's used against them.
b) That in the hands of a woman going through labour an ordinary kitchen implement can become a lethal ninja weapon.

Guidance for men during labour

What a man should **DO during labour**	What a man should **NOT DO during labour**
Pay the mother-to-be undivided attention	The crossword
Offer unwavering encouragement	Nod off
Bring her everything she asks for	Pop out for a 'swift half'
Tell her she's doing really well	Say 'this isn't so bad, is it?'
Play whale music	Play death metal
Play Enya	Play gangsta rap
Offer her nuts, fruit or energy bars	Chow down on a Big Mac meal
Help her shift position when she asks	Say 'this is hard work' while doing so
Give her nitrous oxide when requested	Video himself taking nitrous oxide
Be sympathetic to her screams	Say 'keep it down a bit, love.'
Understand when she gets angry	Say 'chill out, yeah?'
Ignore personal insults during birthing	File them away and brood on them
Change into scrubs if asked	Soap up from hand to elbow
Listen to the doctor's instructions	Say 'I've seen *Casualty*, I know all this'
Ignore her temporary incontinence	Make a face and open the window
Stay the entire time	Ask impatiently 'how much longer?'
Occasionally check for important emails	Take a selfie with his wife
Let her grip his hand as hard as she needs	Say 'ow, that hurts.' Hurts? HURTS?
Stay up near his wife's head	Position himself near the business end
Tell her she looks amazing	Tell her she looks exhausted
Keep his thoughts to himself	Say 'cows don't make this much fuss.'
Keep his thoughts to himself	Tell her he's feeling her pain too
Try and keep it as private as possible	Livestream the birth on Periscope
Turn off the football on TV	Ask if she can wait till full time

Garaging

This is the place where the baby will spend much of their first year. As will you, lying on a hard floor or slumped in a soft chair listening obsessively to their breathing (at least for your first baby: see 'subsidiary vehicles').

You will almost certainly want a baby monitor, which lets you hear if your baby cries when you're downstairs. These used to be more or less glorified walkie-talkies with a tiny range, and you needed to be Usain Bolt to turn them both on at opposite ends of the house before the

connection was lost. Now they have video cameras, thermometers, multiple channels, internet access and probably a subscription to Sky Atlantic and a hotline to the CIA too.

If you go upstairs to check on your baby while you have guests downstairs, do not tell your baby how achingly tedious/self-satisfied/bitchy your guests are. Your baby will neither hear nor understand. Your guests, listening to the baby monitor as though it were the *Today* programme, will do both.

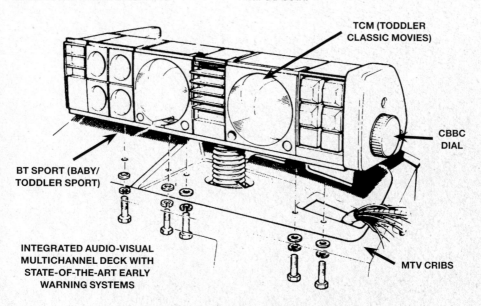

TCM (TODDLER CLASSIC MOVIES)

CBBC DIAL

BT SPORT (BABY/ TODDLER SPORT)

INTEGRATED AUDIO-VISUAL MULTICHANNEL DECK WITH STATE-OF-THE-ART EARLY WARNING SYSTEMS

MTV CRIBS

FIG 1•6 **BABY HOME ENTERTAINMENT SYSTEM**

The nursery

1) Consider using colours that are calming and nurturing. Not for the baby's sake, of course, but for yours. You will need it.

2) Ignore all the too-perfect Pinterest boards showing immaculately tidy nurseries, and save expensive and exquisite decoration schemes for later: your baby will be too young to appreciate them. Take the money and use it for something useful, like a vat of vodka.

3) You will almost certainly have chosen some trinkets and knick-knacks to make the nursery exactly how you want it. These have a place, and the place is inside the nearest drawer. Every flat surface will be packed with changing mats, nappies, wipes, feeding supplies and so on. The last thing you want is a cute little ornament finding its way into a baby's nappy.

4) Invest in a rocking chair. Yes, they're cumbersome and can be uncomfortable, but when your baby is fighting sleep and you're at the end of your tether, the simple act of rocking backwards and forwards can help your baby drop off and thereby preserve your sanity.

5) Control the noise in the nursery. This doesn't mean soundproofing the place – babies will soon sleep through normal household noise – but making sure there aren't unexpected annoying sounds such as creaking floorboards, crashing doors, or your own muffled industrial language when you find you can't get up from the rocking chair without using your hands and you can't use your hands because they're full of sleeping baby....

Nursery positioning

Good
A quiet room near your bedroom so you don't have to go far at night.

Better
A quiet room miles away from your bedroom so someone else can deal with the 3am wake-up calls.

Best
A suite at the nearest five-star hotel while a night nurse takes care of all the baby's needs.

Refuelling

Have you ever noticed that in *Goldilocks and the Three Bears*, Papa Bear's porridge is piping hot, baby's is perfect, and Mama Bear's is stone cold? There's a good reason for that which any new mother will understand pretty quickly.

Much of your attention in the baby's first few months is paid to two things:

a) what's going down and
b) what's coming up.

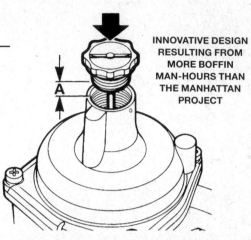

INNOVATIVE DESIGN RESULTING FROM MORE BOFFIN MAN-HOURS THAN THE MANHATTAN PROJECT

FIG 1•7 **ANTI-REFLUX TWIN-VALVE BOTTLE TEAT SYSTEM**

Stages of feeding

Birth – 3 months
Milk (breast or formula).

Signs of readiness: locks onto dispensing unit like a Eurofighter's missile guidance system.

4–6 months
Starting on pureed food (fruit, vegetables and meat).

Signs of readiness: can hold head up, makes chewing motions, closes mouth around a spoon, clicks fingers for waiter, demands menu, listens attentively to specials list.

7–9 months
Starting on solid food (soft cheese, scrambled egg, crackers, well-cooked pasta).

Signs of readiness: picks up objects with thumb and forefinger, transfers items from hand to hand, puts everything in his mouth, sends food back for being undercooked, peruses wine list, asks whether service is included.

4–5 years
Suddenly realises spoons don't actually sound like aeroplanes.

Breast and bottle feeding

Bottle feeding

If you bottle feed, you will be a total zealot about sterilisation, using plastic tweezers to handle perfectly sterilised bottles, teats and lids with the dexterity of a keyhole surgeon. At some stage, however, you will realise you can just slam them all in the dishwasher for just the same result (and perhaps with an added twist of lemon depending on your choice of 3-in-1 tablet). For subsequent babies, if a bottle falls on the floor you'll wipe the teat on your shirt or suck it a moment before resuming the feed – see Subsidiary vehicles.

What goes down...

Since what goes down must come up (Newton's Fourth Law of Thermodynamics/Spock's First Law of Infant Feeding), your baby will be sick on you sooner or later. If you want to hurry the process, put on a nice top. Babies have some sort of weird sixth sense about these things. Fathers leaving for work in smart suits have been known to shimmy down the drainpipe rather than cuddle a recently fed baby for fear that they will be attending the board meeting sporting a stain that looks like a map of Australia and smells like rotten curd.

Breastfeeding

The etiquette of breastfeeding remains tricky. Not in private, obviously, but some people are still uncomfortable to see a woman breastfeeding in public. How you react depends on precisely the location you're in:

1) If you're in a shopping mall, park yourself outside the nearest Agent Provocateur and point out to anyone who takes issue that you're showing quite a lot less naked flesh than the pouting model on the advertising hoardings in the shop window.

2) If you're at a family gathering, be prepared for your father-in-law to splutter into his G&T and engage you in stilted conversation about the dreadful weather for this time of year.

When your baby has drunk enough, he may well pass out on the bar, still in situ. This is excellent practice for his university years.

Emission control

As adults we don't think much about poo, with the obvious exceptions involving any or all of Delhi, Montezuma, belly and revenge. But once you have a baby, you have to deal with more poo than the Thames Water sewage department.

Your first close encounter of the turd kind will be meconium. This is neither an obscure element on the periodic table nor a waste product of nuclear fission, though there will be times when either might seem plausible. Meconium is a mixture of amniotic fluid, mucus and other stuff that the baby's ingested in the womb, and it looks like what road crews use to resurface the M3 with.

For the first few days it's all that comes out of your baby's backside. It's odourless, so enjoy it while you can. Because it's not long before meconium gives way to the real deal, and then you're in a whole world of hurt.

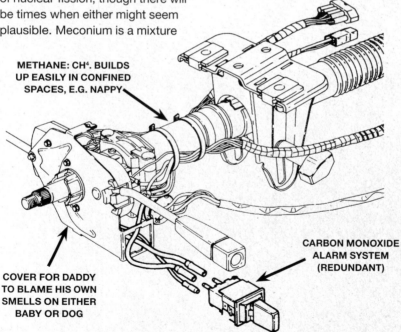

METHANE: CH⁴. BUILDS UP EASILY IN CONFINED SPACES, E.G. NAPPY

COVER FOR DADDY TO BLAME HIS OWN SMELLS ON EITHER BABY OR DOG

CARBON MONOXIDE ALARM SYSTEM (REDUNDANT)

FIG 1•8 **EMISSIONS CONTROL – REDUCING HARMFUL GASES**

Things to look out for...

Velocity and frequency

Baby poo can cause a rip in the space-time continuum, a glitch in the Matrix and a disturbance in the Force. Not only can babies poo round the clock, but the lengths they can achieve with projectile poo have to be seen to be believed. Pacing out the distance between the changing mat and the explosion on the wall is like walking the world long jump record at Ripley's Believe It Or Not. And that's when they're not wearing a nappy. If they are, all that force is directed upwards, coating their back in several layers of whatever...

Colour is on the menu

Checking the colour of your baby's poo is a cross between ancient sorcerers reading entrails and modern interior designers perusing the Farrow & Ball paint chart. Your baby is verily the Picasso of poo.

Dijon and cottage cheese yellow:
Normal breastfed

Peanut butter brown:
Normal formula feed.

Milk chocolate brown:
Normal once started on solid foods.

Poos of interest

1) The 10 Minutes Before Daddy Gets Home Poo
It's twice as smelly and four times as messy as usual. Daddy will be home in 10 minutes, and the moment he gets in he can clean it up.

2) The Bathtime Floater
There are two kinds of parents – those who admit their kids have done a poo in the bath, and those who lie.

3) The Post-Constipation Poo
The only thing worse than a baby pooing is a baby not pooing. Constipation can go on for days, replete with straining, crying and diabolical sulphur smells. When the dam is finally breached it's like a mushroom cloud off a Pacific atoll.

WARNING

Whatever you do, don't try and wrap a bathtime floater in toilet paper. The paper just disintegrates in the water and makes it ten times worse.

Pit stops

You may swear before you give birth that you will never lift a baby in the air and sniff their nappy to see whether there's a poo there. But you will. Everyone does eventually. Maybe that's why rugby lineouts come so naturally to players: because at some neural level they remember being propelled skywards by strong hands around their waist (though the smell in an international rugby scrum is many times worse than anything a dozen babies could conjure up).

Nappy changing

Changing a baby's nappy is rather like a Formula One team's pit stop:

1) A huge number of tasks to be crammed into a very short space of time.
2) Split-second accuracy is of the essence if disaster is to be avoided.
3) Specialist equipment needed.

Like Murray Walker, you may well find yourself shouting 'GO, GO, GO!' as the process is successfully completed (though when F1 pitstops go wrong, Lewis Hamilton doesn't tend to wee in your face).

STATE-OF-THE-ART SENSORS ENSURE SPLIT-SECOND TIMING

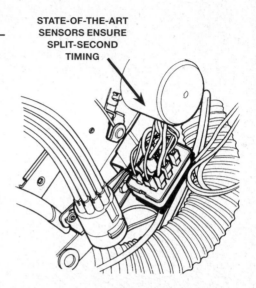

FIG 1•9 **SMOOTH OPERATION REQUIRES FULLY INTEGRATED SYSTEMS**

It gets better...

Soon you will have everything to hand like a well-prepared surgeon: changing mat here, cotton wool there, barrier cream, clean nappy, plastic bag, clean clothes and all the rest. Your hands will be a well-practised blur of efficiency, you will happily sing to your baby while changing them, and you will wonder how you ever made such a Horlicks of it to start with.

⚠ Changing a baby's nappy

Nappy changes should be slick, quick and efficient.
Your first attempt is unlikely to be any of those three.

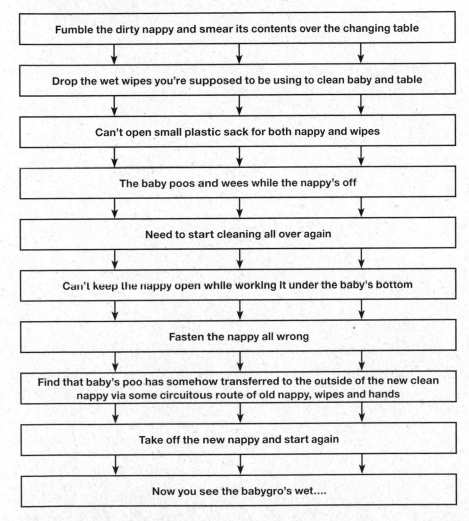

Fumble the dirty nappy and smear its contents over the changing table

↓

Drop the wet wipes you're supposed to be using to clean baby and table

↓

Can't open small plastic sack for both nappy and wipes

↓

The baby poos and wees while the nappy's off

↓

Need to start cleaning all over again

↓

Can't keep the nappy open while working it under the baby's bottom

↓

Fasten the nappy all wrong

↓

Find that baby's poo has somehow transferred to the outside of the new clean nappy via some circuitous route of old nappy, wipes and hands

↓

Take off the new nappy and start again

↓

Now you see the babygro's wet....

Reactions

A baby will elicit a whole range of reactions from your family, friends and colleagues. Some of them will cry hysterically. Others will come round literally hours after you return home from hospital and drink all your wine while you stare bleary-eyed at them while silently chanting 'please... just... piss... off' over and over again. Some will make their own monogrammed presents. A grandmother – especially one who has just become one for the first time – will let out a scream of joy which will be heard around the world.

Of course, reactions begin much earlier, when you first discover you're pregnant. For the father, here's a list of how to react to the news:

Bad reaction	*Good reaction*
Are you sure?	*That's great!*
How did that happen?	*That's great!*
Whose is it?	*That's great!*
Already?	*That's great!*
[Silence]	*That's great!*

THE LINE OF SANITY RESISTANCE

THE KNIFE OF GOOD INTENTIONS

FIG 1•10 **THE CAN OF WORMS – OPEN AT YOUR PERIL**

Choosing a name
When choosing the baby's name, do not involve your families. It's hard enough finding a name you both like without throwing more opinions into the mix. Any common name will be dismissed as boring, and any unusual one as weird. Obscure family names will be put up for discussion. You'll end up conducting the kind of up-all-night-end-at-five-in-the-morning multiparty negotiations that are usually the preserve of global climate change summits, and you'll be getting plenty enough sleepless nights as it is once the baby comes. No point starting early. Tell everyone the baby's name when it arrives and leave them to like it or lump it.

⚠ Stupid things people say

What people say	Response
Is he a good baby?	Good is a relativist moral construct
Does he sleep through the night?	Only if I get the dosage just right
Are you getting much sleep?	LOOK AT ME! WHAT DO YOU THINK?
Have you got a routine?	Am I wearing military uniform?
He looks just like you	So I'm puffy-faced and half-bald?
He looks just like his dad	Let's hope so for all our sakes
You're breastfeeding, right?	Back off with your judgmentalism
What's that white stuff on your shirt?	Puke. Of course.
Cherish every moment	Thank you, Ms Platitude
Back when I had children...	*smile sweetly, zone out*
Is that a birth mark?	No. I split some Chianti on his head.
Is he crawling yet?	He's 8 weeks old, not Superman.
Are you going back to work?	Yes, because I need the money
You shouldn't go back to work	Does this look like 1952 to you?
It'll get easier	If I had £1 for every time that...
He's so small	Thanks for making me worry
He's so big	Thanks for making me worry
She looks like a hamster	You're no oil painting yourself
Is it a boy or a girl?	Head-to-toe pink. Take a wild guess.
How was the birth?	Shall I ask you something personal?
Lucky you, having a C-section	What's your definition of unlucky?
When are you having another?	You want to come and watch?
Are you getting much help?	My husband isn't always in the pub.
I understand. We have a puppy	Go away.
Can I do anything?	Yes. Stop asking dumb questions.

Transportation methods

The golden rule of babies is this: the smaller they are, the more stuff they need. A ten-minute trip down the road with a newborn looks like Napoleon's retreat from Moscow.

There are more slings and backpacks on the market than you can shake a stick at, but the most basic item of baby transport remains the pram.

The pram

So you have your pram. In the shop before the baby was born, when you could still remember what a good night's sleep was like, it all looked easy: pull this lever to collapse, push that button to expand.

Now, a few days into parenthood and desperate for some time out of the house, you try it.

Push that button. Trap your finger. Strain your back while trying to free trapped finger with other hand. Expand pram. Put baby in pram. Find pram won't fit through door. Take baby out. Half-collapse pram and force it through doorway. Pick up baby (now screaming) and go through door. Realise you forgot to put brake on pram. Watch pram roll down street. Hurry to catch pram before it rolls into road and causes multiple pile-up. Put baby in pram. Fasten straps round baby. Feel the first drops of rain. Have existential crisis.

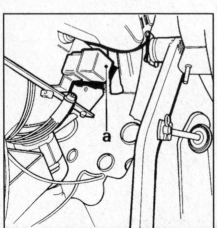 

FIG 1•11 **PRAM PINCER POINTS. SEVERED FINGERS JUST OUT OF SHOT**

Public transport

Public transport provides its own set of challenges. Train and bus passengers find many things annoying, but these five are probably on most people's lists.

5) Armrest hogs.
4) Tinny music coming through headphones.
3) Eating takeaway curries or pungent pasties.
2) Loud mobile phone conversations
1) Crying babies.

If your baby starts crying, you will hear every sigh of disapproval and sense every eye-roll burning into the back of your head. And flights are a whole different circle of hell altogether. Sometimes babys are as good as gold; sometimes they're not. Sometimes they try to throw peanuts at all and sundry.

In Norse mythology the god Freyr had a magical boat called Skidbladnir, which could be folded up to fit in a pocket. The pram manufacturer who could do the same would soon retire rich.

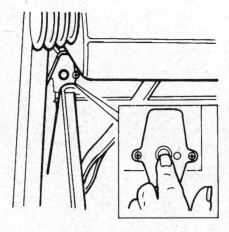

FIG 1•12 **NOT THE ON-OFF BUTTON: THE LOUD-LOUDER BUTTON**

It's worse for you

No matter how annoying a crying baby is, it's far worse for you, trying to control him, than for anyone else. As long as you're doing your best to soothe the baby, to hell with them all. You've paid for your ticket and you're never going to see any of them again.

Besides, at least your baby isn't getting drunk, panicking, shouting 'we're all going to die!', hitting on stewardesses or starting fights. So even a screaming baby is a more desirable travelling companion than half all regular travellers.

Running-in

The baby's development is rapid and takes place in three main areas: motor skills, language and social/emotional development. The milestones listed (progress by months) can vary greatly between babies, though this makes precious little difference in later life. Nonetheless, few things cause more competitiveness among parents than how advanced their infants are.

'Crispian's only four months old, but he can already drive a golf ball 250 yards straight off the tee.'

'Really? He sounds a little backward, if you'll forgive my bluntness. Amelia recited The Rime Of The Ancient Mariner in its entirety the other day, and she's just 11 weeks old.'

Parents tell more lies on behalf of their children than men do about their golf handicaps or women do about not minding that someone else has got exactly the same outfit.

Your child is not backward. He may not be composing symphonies like a 3-year-old Mozart but nor are any of his classmates.

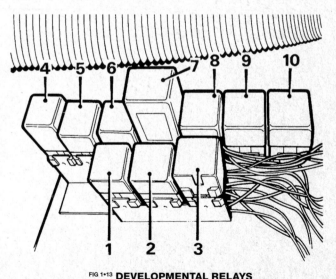

FIG 1•13 **DEVELOPMENTAL RELAYS**

1   *PUSH-UPS*
2   *CRAWLING*
3   *CLIMBING*
4   *BABBLING*
5   *TALKING*
6   *DEMANDING*
7   *MIMICKING*
8   *PEEKABOO*
9   *SIT-IN PROTESTS*
10 *TANTRUMS*

Development milestones

Motor skills

3 months
Your baby will be able to lift his head and chest while on his tummy, and will soon be doing the mini push-ups that look more like a turtle trying to right itself than anything you might see at military boot camp.

7–8 months
Your baby will be able to sit unaided and grasp at objects such as his toys, your nose and the dog's tail. By one year the baby may be standing unaided and will be able to get around by crawling or yogic bum-shuffling.

12–24 months
Once your baby can walk unaided, the world is his oyster and your nightmare. Stairs, sofas, beds, chairs, tables and shelves become obstacle courses of which the SAS would be proud.

Language skills

3 months
Your baby will be starting to babble and mimic the sounds you're making (when you speak, that is, not when you weep copiously or demand gin with a hissed urgency).

7–8 months
Your baby will be laughing and 'talking' to you, which may sound a little too like the kind of conversations you have in the pub after several pints for comfort.

12–24 months
By 12 months you may hear his first words, which statistically are more likely to be 'dada' rather than 'mama', the ungrateful little blighter.

Social and emotional skills

3 months
Your baby will be enjoying playtime and imitating your facial expressions, which will almost certainly make you think of Les Dawson.

7–8 months
Your baby will be very keen on playing Peekaboo, again and again and a-sodding-gain, and also on looking at himself in the nearest mirror.

12–24 months
Your baby will want to do everything themself while imitating things you do, such as talking on the phone. If he yells into the phone non-stop you may wish to improve your phone manner.

Routine maintenance

Your baby will get sick sooner or later. This is the bad news. The good news is that most illnesses are short, mild and easily contained. Colds, colic, reflux and even ear infections usually pass, though there'll be some world-class grizzling along the way. But enough of your response. Your baby will probably be pretty unhappy too.

There are many possible signs of illness, but your baby's behaviour is the best indication of how they're feeling. If it's different from usual or worrying in any way, take them to the doctor. Trust your instincts.

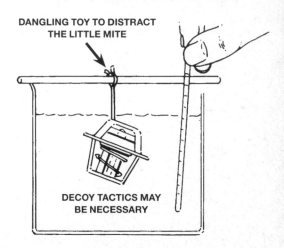

DANGLING TOY TO DISTRACT THE LITTLE MITE

DECOY TACTICS MAY BE NECESSARY

FIG 1•14 **TAKING BABY'S TEMPERATURE**

Parent well/baby well **Situation normal**	*Parent ill/baby well* **An unadulterated nightmare**
Proceed as usual.	You want to be left alone to sleep and watch *Trisha*. Your baby wants to party like it's 1999. Good luck. You'll need it.
Parent well/baby ill **Worrying but usually temporary**	*Parent ill/baby ill* **You can both feel grotty together**
Once you know the illness isn't severe, you may – whisper it quietly – be grateful that the baby sleeps more than usual, giving you some rest.	Cuddle up and demand that Daddy/husband waits on you both hand and foot.

⚠️ Vaccinations

Vaccinations can cause much trepidation among parents but again are entirely routine. (There is an anti-vaxxer movement, which may or may not include those who also believe the moon landings were faked, 9/11 was an inside job and that the Duke of Edinburgh is a 12-foot lizard alien overlord.)

The less fuss you make of the vaccination, the less likely your baby is to find it distressing. Sit them on your lap, distract them during the injection itself, and give them a gold star for bravery afterwards.

Doctors

Your baby may find the doctor suspicious or give him the evils. The doctor may point out that he didn't go through seven years of medical school just for this. The nurse will probably side with your baby, since nurses tend to have a similarly low opinion of doctors. The doctor may then storm off in a huff or suggest you have a go if you think it's so easy. When your baby's grown up, you may or may not choose to tell him that he unwittingly cast the first stone in the destruction of the NHS.

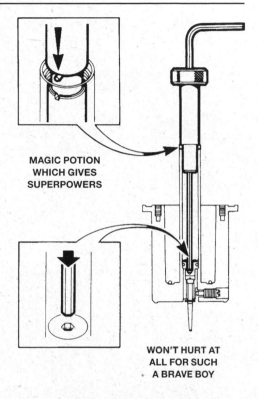

MAGIC POTION
WHICH GIVES
SUPERPOWERS

WON'T HURT AT
ALL FOR SUCH
A BRAVE BOY

FIG 1•15 **WAYS OF GETTING YOUR BABY
THROUGH THE INJECTIONS**

Parents may also voluntarily inject themselves with small doses of something harmful. In their case, it's called Botox.

Night-time storage

Ah, sleep. It's just something you take for granted more or less up to the moment you have a baby. Up all night on the sauce or to get lucky? Nothing that a massive cappuccino and a full English can't fix.

Once the baby's arrived, however, you count every minute of sleep and would pay the riches of Croesus for every minute more.

Adjusting

In the first few days of your baby's life, she may spend much of the day asleep. Do not be lulled into a false sense of security. As the sun sets behind the horizon, her eyes will pop open and she will transform into a mentalist vampire, demanding to be fed, burped, cuddled and soothed till the break of dawn.

Even when you foist on her the concept of night and day, she will continue to have worse timekeeping than the Italians until she's at least three or four months old. She will sleep when she likes and wake when she likes, and in the short term there's not much you can do about it. If you work for the police force and your baby refuses to take a nap, then you can – wait for it – charge her with resisting a rest.

GENTLY DOES IT: GETTING BABY OFF TO SLEEP

BABY-WAKING RATCHET. NEVER FAILS

THE SWEET SPOT WHERE YOU BOTH SLEEP

FIG 1•16 COUNTING EVERY MINUTE

You can guarantee that
a) Everyone will have advice on how to get your baby sleeping properly
b) That advice will be contradictory. Don't let your baby sleep too long; never wake a sleeping baby. Stick to a routine; don't let a routine take over your life. Don't sleep with them; put them in your bed.

Basically, do whatever works. Don't read books (apart from this one, of course): read your baby.

Perpetual motion machine

If you want to get your baby to sleep and nothing else seems to be working, sing Metallica's 'Nothing Else Matters' to them. Seriously. 100% success rate.

Total sample: me and my mate Sean. But it did work for all four of our kids. (That's two each, not four for him and me together, because… ah, never mind.)

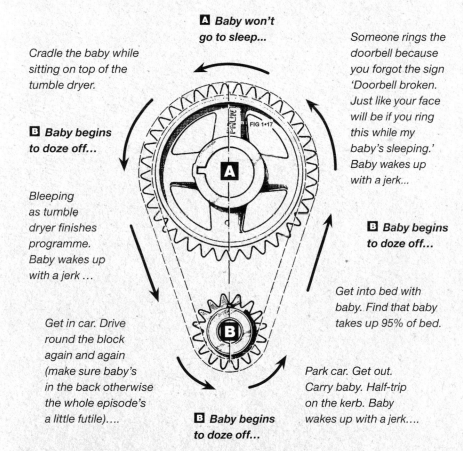

A *Baby won't go to sleep...*

Cradle the baby while sitting on top of the tumble dryer.

B *Baby begins to doze off...*

Bleeping as tumble dryer finishes programme. Baby wakes up with a jerk ...

Get in car. Drive round the block again and again (make sure baby's in the back otherwise the whole episode's a little futile)....

Someone rings the doorbell because you forgot the sign 'Doorbell broken. Just like your face will be if you ring this while my baby's sleeping.' Baby wakes up with a jerk...

B *Baby begins to doze off...*

Get into bed with baby. Find that baby takes up 95% of bed.

Park car. Get out. Carry baby. Half-trip on the kerb. Baby wakes up with a jerk....

B *Baby begins to doze off...*

In-car entertainment

The one thing your baby won't be short of is toys. Every grandparent, godparent, friend and colleague will want to give the nipper a little present. Some will be expensive and some cheap, some beautiful and some hideous, some robust and some fragile. And chances are your baby won't be interested in 90% of them.

Most babies are quite happy to sit in the middle of what looks like the set for *Toy Story 4* and ignore the lot in favour of an empty water bottle, a tissue box or a DVD case.

If they do focus on a specific toy, chances are it'll be as much for the tag or washing label on the bottom as anything else.

Simple things...
You can keep your baby entertained for weeks just with ordinary things found in the kitchen: plastic cups, egg boxes, wooden spoons and so on. Think of it as a feature-length episode of *Blue Peter* – what the heck was sticky-back plastic anyway? – and you won't go far wrong.

... and expensive things
At the other end of the scale, of course, your baby will find particular fascination with things that are fantastically expensive such as your smartphone. They will enjoy testing said smartphone's resistance to being dropped on the kitchen floor and/or down the toilet.

ROTOR UNIT. BELOVED BY BLOWER FANS AND BABIES ALIKE

BEST TO DISCONNECT BEFOREHAND

FIG 1•18 **FAN MOTOR UNIT – BETTER THAN TOYS TEN TIMES THE PRICE**

WARNING

Baby rice is good for babies. Brown rice is good for drying out your mobile phone when your baby has dropped it in the bath.

Bath time

Just as your bath is not complete without certain accoutrements – bath salts, candles, large glass of Chardonnay – neither is your baby's (though without the Chardonnay). In later years, when the baby has become a teenager (see *HAYNES EXPLAINS: TEENAGERS*), a garden hose applied very cold at high pressure is the best way to wash them, but at this stage gentler methods are required.

Having ascertained that the water is like Goldilocks' porridge, neither too hot nor too cold, make sure the following are to hand:

1) Baby shampoo, in order to make baby Mohican

2) Baby bubble bath, in order to make baby beard and baby Afro

3) Rubber and plastic bath toys, preferably (a) slightly mildewed (b) set up to allow games at which you can be Competitive Parent and win. Life's a competition, remember, and it's never too early to teach your child to deal with losing.

4) Bathtub crayons which wash off. Not to be confused with permanent marker pens

5) DIY Jacuzzi maker (see 'emission control' section)

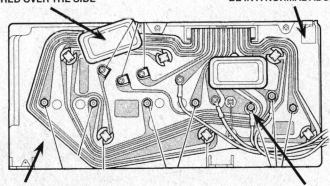

HALF A SWIMMING POOL'S WORTH SLOSHED OVER THE SIDE

WHERE THE CHARDONNAY WOULD BE IN A NORMAL ADULT BATH

PATH OF LEAST RESISTANCE FOR SAID WATER TO COLLAPSE CEILING BELOW

LOW-FLYING OBJECTS HURLED AT PARENT'S HEAD

FIG 1•19 **A TYPICAL BABY BATH SCENE**

Subsidiary vehicles

The care and attention you lavish on your first-born is all-consuming. When you have a second baby, you will find yourself much less obsessive. By the time you get to your third or fourth, it'll be all you can do to remember their name, though you may be vaguely aware there are more small people living in your house than you had previously thought.

But all this is in the dim and distant future when you are in the throes of PFBS – Precious First-Born Syndrome.

Having your first baby is a little like having a new car. They both have a particular smell (not the same smell, obviously), they both seem bright and shiny, you take excessive care with both of them, and so on.

A couple of years down the line, when that car is less new and there's another baby, you'll be much more lax about it all. A few knocks and bangs, a bit more dirt, and guess what? They both still work fine.

Probably best to keep the fluffy dice, the blue neon underlighting and the spinner wheels just to the car, though.

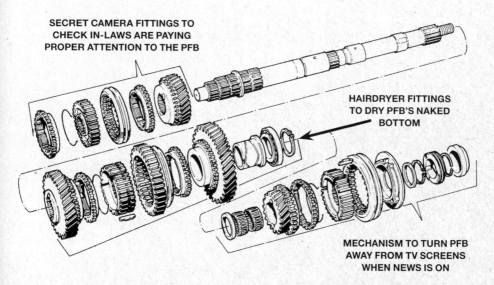

SECRET CAMERA FITTINGS TO CHECK IN-LAWS ARE PAYING PROPER ATTENTION TO THE PFB

HAIRDRYER FITTINGS TO DRY PFB'S NAKED BOTTOM

MECHANISM TO TURN PFB AWAY FROM TV SCREENS WHEN NEWS IS ON

FIG 1•20 **ALL-PURPOSE 3-IN-1 GADGET TO MAINTAIN PRECIOUSNESS**

Precious First-Born Syndrome (PFBS)

The following are real examples from sufferers. Thankfully they have all recovered sufficiently to laugh about it.

1) Using yellow and black tape to map a path out of the baby's bedroom to avoid creaking floorboards.

2) Warming cucumber sticks in the microwave for fear they would hurt the baby if served cold.

3) Carrying the baby bath – full – through the house to the warmest room so the baby wasn't exposed to cool air even for a second, and of course soaking the carpets in the process.

4) Writing out the lyrics of the baby's 'favourite song' for the babysitter and making her sing it to check she knew the tune.

5) Printing and laminating six sides of single-spaced instructions for the baby's grandmother.

6) Leaning in close to hear a sleeping baby's breathing, giving her a nudge to make sure, then another nudge just to be on the safe side, and so on till she actually woke up.

7) Testing the 'No More Tears' shampoo by putting some in their own eyes.

8) Bringing sterilised scissors in a Ziploc bag to open formula milk cartons.

9) Painstakingly hand-painting individual treasure map invitations to a pirate-themed birthday party.

10) Ringing the hospital A&E, crying hysterically, because a friend with a slight cough had held the baby for five minutes.

Of course, all these examples are also part of the learning curve that all new parents go through: you so want to do your best for your baby that you can easily end up overdoing it.

WARNING

Most PFBs grow up to be perfectly normal. Some of them, however, may demand that people wait on them hand and foot even in adulthood. These people are called politicans.

⚠ Fault diagnosis

Fault	Diagnosis	Treatment
Baby is crying.	Seems to be hungry.	Come on. This one's obvious. Time to open the milk bar again.
Baby is crying.	Seems to have suffered a minor bang.	Apply Peppa Pig bandage and kiss it better. A couple of kisses will do, but you'll probably still be going at 237.
Baby is crying.	Has nappy rash.	Apply nappy cream. Try to get more of it on the baby's bottom than (a) your hands (b) the floor.
Baby is crying.	Has wind.	Burp the baby. Be prepared for – woah, too late. Another shirt for the wash.
Baby is crying.	Wants company.	Settle in for a night in the chair or on the floor.
Baby is crying.	Over-stimulated.	Maybe wait a few more years before showing him *Star Wars* again.
Baby is crying.	Colic.	Gripe water. If you haven't got any, both baby's griping and yours will go interstellar.
Bad smell in the room. Baby's nappy empty.	Blame the dog.	Put the dog out into the garden.
Bad smell in the room. Baby's nappy empty. Do not own a dog.	Your husband went for a curry last night.	Put your husband out into the garden.
Baby is not crying.	You call that a fault? That, my friend, is nirvana.	Enjoy it while you can. Probably by sleeping.

Conclusion

Thank you for reading HAYNES EXPLAINS: BABIES. We hope the idea of newly minted parenthood is a little less daunting now (though of course it's entirely possible that the opposite is now the case).

Don't worry. A lot of people substantially less intelligent than you have managed to (a) understand American football (b) carry off this parenthood lark without too much mishap. How hard can it really be?

At the end of the day, babies just want what adults do – to be fed, watered and loved. When you lie on the sofa with your tiny baby curled up like a little frog on your chest, heart to heart, the world suddenly makes sense. Being a parent is an enormous privilege, raising these tiny little creatures who are blank canvasses but also very much their own people.

So, although being told to 'cherish

Babies make your days shorter, your nights longer, your bank balance smaller, your floors stickier and your house dirtier. Amazingly, you will still love them.

When your baby starts to misbehave, you can use a playpen. Playpens are nice and safe. When your baby's calmed down, you can climb out again.

the moment' is hugely annoying, it's also true. Babies don't answer back. They mean that your house is filled with more presents than you know what to do with. Having a baby with you means that strangers smile at you in the street without necessarily being deranged, charity collectors, tourists about to ask for directions, or all the above.

No matter how huge your child grows, no matter what they do with their lives and no matter how many children of their own they eventually have, they will always, always, be your baby. This of course won't embarrass them in the slightest when you remind them of this or produce photographic evidence by way of proof. If you don't believe us, try it sometime. They won't bat an eyelid.

We hope you enjoyed this book as much as we enjoyed writing it. More importantly, we hope you enjoy your children's babyhood. There really is nothing like it.

Titles in the Haynes Explains series

Now that Haynes has explained Babies, you can progress to our full-size manuals on car maintenance (less messy than babies), the *Baby Manual* (the serious approach), *Men's Cooking Manual* (hunter, gatherer and chef), *Beer Manual* (to accompany the hunting, gathering and cooking) and *Home Extension Manual* (enough said).

There are Haynes manuals on just about everything – but let us know if we've missed one.

Haynes.com